The Medicine Wheel is a symbol of hope — a movement toward healing for those who seek it. Lulu's wisdom and insight offer the reader an opportunity to explore an intimate inward journey with the Medicine Wheel's deeper meanings, its circular shape, its furred and feathered Spirit Guides and its Seven Directions.

Shahara Redbird, Rainbow Medicine Woman

This book brings to life Native American traditions enriched by nature. Loved Luella's journey to the Native American Medicine Wheel. The book becomes inspirational, devotional and motivational as she describes the Medicine Wheel directions and symbols with respect and honor to our Native American people. A good path to follow. AHO!

Mary Meier, President of St. Kateri Circle
St. Lawrence Martyr Catholic Church
Redondo Beach, California

THE SEVEN DIRECTIONS OF THE
MEDICINE WHEEL

THE SEVEN DIRECTIONS OF THE MEDICINE WHEEL

A practical guide for everyday living based on Native American teachings

Luella Wagner

Woodland Hills, California

The Seven Directions of the Medicine Wheel
A practical guide for everyday living based on Native American teachings
First Edition

© 2021 Luella Wagner, All Rights Reserved
Snow Crocus Publishing
www.snowcrocuspublishing.com
Woodland Hills, California

Publisher's Cataloging-in-Publication data

Names: Wagner, Luella, author.
Title: The seven directions of the medicine wheel : a practical guide for everyday living based on Native American teachings / Luella Wagner.
Description: Woodland Hills, CA: Snow Crocus Publishing, 2021.
Identifiers: LCCN: 2021910626 | ISBN: 978-1-7364209-3-5 (hardcover) | 978-1-7364209-0-4 (paperback) | 978-1-7364209-1-1 (ebook) | 978-1-7364209-2-8 (audiobook)
Subjects: LCSH Indians of North America--Religion. | Indian philosophy--North America. | Medicine wheels. | Conduct of life. | BISAC BODY, MIND & SPIRIT / Inspiration & Personal Growth | SELF-HELP / Spiritual | SELF-HELP / Motivational & Inspirational
Classification: LCC BL624 .W34 2021 | DDC 299/.7--dc23

Illustrator: Julia Hanna
Editor: Adele Field
Graphic Designs: Gretchen Dorris

*Dedicated to Julie, Tiger,
Juanita, and MooMoo,
my beloved animals
who have guided me continually
on my life's journey.*

CONTENTS

FOREWORD

There is a Native American saying: "Before you judge another, you must walk one mile in that person's moccasins." When Luella Wagner stepped out of the U-Haul onto the soil of Montana, she planted her feet firmly in the moccasins of the Native American people who have lived on that land for thousands of years.

She entered into and absorbed the culture and wisdom that greeted her there. Although she no longer lives and works there, the dreams and hopes, the struggles, the joys, the knowledge and gifts of the Native people have become hers. The blood that runs through their veins now courses through her own. She went to Montana to teach the people there and found that they became her teachers and mentors.

She has left the reservation and now comes to us bringing with her a wealth of knowledge and wisdom for daily living. Her practical approach to the teachings and the beautiful illustrations bring the Wheel and its wisdom to life. Luella has taken a deep dive into the journey of the Medicine Wheel and shares with us the vast riches of this powerful tool for personal transformation.

As you open the pages of this book you will be invited to remove your shoes, for you are on Sacred Ground, and step into the moccasins of our Native American sisters and brothers. May your journey, like hers, be a blessing for you that will inspire you to share that blessing with others. Aho!

> *Sr. Chris Machado*
> *Executive Director*
> *Holy Spirit Retreat Center*

ACKNOWLEDGMENTS

I owe a sincere debt of gratitude to a close number of friends who made this book possible.

Dolores Freeman, who gave me and my three cats a ride up to the reservation in a U-Haul for what was the beginning of a lifetime journey that I am still traveling.

Adele Field, who over the years has been a constant source of inspiration, motivation, and encouragement. She has used her editing skills to shine, polish, and make my words ready for the world. When I got the idea to write a book about the Medicine Wheel, my first inclination was to visit the Big Horn Medicine Wheel at Big Horn National Forest in Wyoming and experience it firsthand. Adele happily came along. She literally has been with me every step of the way.

Julia Hanna, my former student at Immaculate Heart High School, who is now studying to be a veterinarian, for her colorful animal illustrations that make my words come alive.

Gretchen Dorris, who did a superb job on the graphic designs for the interior and the cover, and captured the essence of the Medicine Wheel exactly.

The staff at Holy Spirit Retreat Center in Encino, who gave me the opportunity to present numerous retreats and workshops on the Medicine Wheel at the Center. My workshops and retreats provided the groundwork for this book.

The members of the Kateri Circle, who have welcomed me into their community and have allowed me to share in their rich spiritual tradition.

Grey Wolf, who sparked my interest in Native American culture and spirituality long before I went to the reservation.

Joe Vasquez and his wife Redbird, who have inspired me to continue in my Medicine Wheel journey over the years.

Skye McKenzie, Diane Ventura, Gay Hennessy, and the entire TOR staff who have been a constant source of encouragement and have supported me in numerous ways over the years.

Reese Abbene, who invited me to bring the Medicine Wheel to Notre Dame High School in Sherman Oaks.

Gina Finer, who gave me numerous opportunities to share my knowledge of the Medicine Wheel at Immaculate Heart Middle School in Los Angeles.

Toni Casala, for the tremendous opportunities she gave me as I continued my writing adventure.

Karen Dabby, for her creative spirit and multiple talents that have inspired my work immensely.

This book would not have been possible without the generosity of those mentioned above.

A portion of sales proceeds of this book go to
Native American communities.

Big Horn Medicine Wheel
Big Horn National Forest, Wyoming

MY INTRODUCTION TO THE MEDICINE WHEEL

Several years ago, I lost my teaching job and with the unemployment rate then at 12% in my state of California, I went into a panic. I sent out resumes all over the country and the only school I heard back from was a little tiny Indian school in southeastern Montana. So I packed up a U-Haul and headed to the reservation. Negative zero-degree temperatures, no car, no internet, no Starbucks; it was the best thing that could have happened to me!

When I came back from the reservation, many people were interested in my experience, so I began giving presentations at local, state, and national conferences. During my presentations, I found that there was a particular interest in the Native American Medicine Wheel. I had heard of the Medicine Wheel while on the reservation, but it still remained a mystery to me. I then set out to learn as much as I possibly could about this ancient spiritual tool.

I wanted to have the full-on experience of the Medicine Wheel, so I ventured back to Montana, where I met my friend Adele, and we set our sights on the Big Horn Medicine Wheel in Big Horn National Forest in Wyoming. We left Billings, made a few stops for food along the way, got on the highway to Sheridan, and then headed through the winding roads of Wyoming until we finally arrived at the Big Horn Medicine Wheel. Even though it was August, we bundled up as though it was the middle of winter. It is never warm at the Medicine Wheel even during the summer months. The Medicine Wheel is only open from May to September, since snow typically covers it October through April.

We parked our car in the lot marked for visitors, but we still had a bit of a hike ahead of us. We stopped at a small cabin adjacent to the parking lot where a woman welcomed us to the site and handed us a few brochures. A wide footpath led to the wheel. As we began our trek up to the site we encountered several others who were on their way back down. Once we reached the top of Medicine Mountain, it was enveloped in a mist, a cloud of sorts. High above the world, I looked out towards the horizon and took in the majesty of the scenery.

At an elevation of nearly 10,000 feet there was a definite mystical presence surrounding the wheel. I felt "above it all"— above all my own personal woes and tribulations, above all the world's problems and predicaments. There was no feeling of stress on Medicine Wheel Mountain. There was only calmness and serenity.

Our timing was auspicious since there had been a ritual there earlier in the day and the lingering effects made our experience even more sublime. It was very quiet; only one other person was circumambulating the wheel. Adele and I walked around the wheel in contemplation and reflection. Knowing that I was standing on sacred ground with an ancient tool that Natives have revered for centuries gave me a very deep appreciation and respect for their ways.

The wheel itself, its size and the arrangement of the stones, its location in relation to the sun, and its remote setting all contributed to a new and different experience for me. I thought of all the places I had visited in foreign countries, while here in my own country existed a simple, yet deeply profound sacred spot that held the wisdom of the ages.

Medicine Wheel spokes are often in alignment with the stars and the location of the sunrise and the sunset. The Big Horn Medicine Wheel is approximately 80 feet in diameter. At the very center of the wheel is a mound of stones, or cairn. Radiating out from the cairn are 28 stone spokes that connect with a series of other stones making up the outer circle. The 28 spokes correlate with the lunar calendar. There are five smaller stone circles situated at various points around the circumference with a sixth stone circle outside the circumference, yet connected to the wheel by one of the spokes.

Adele and I circled the fence that surrounded and protected the Medicine Wheel. Prayer cloths of many shapes, sizes, and colors were hung on the fence, holding the prayers of those who left them there, adding to the sacredness of the site. The gentle breeze that permeated the grounds carried the prayer intentions across the horizon to another dimension.

I'm not sure how long we stayed at the Medicine Wheel. There was no sense of time. There was no pressure to "hurry up" for the next person in line. Time for a moment stood still, but as the sun began to set, a chill in the air let us know that we had been there long enough and it was time to leave. Walking back I felt an immediate sense of peace and tranquility, yet I knew that I would experience the effects of the Medicine Wheel for a long time to come.

When I came home to California I continued my study of the Medicine Wheel. I read numerous books and articles and I participated in several Medicine Wheel ceremonies. I discovered that there are numerous interpretations of the Medicine Wheel, yet they all share the same basic teaching that humanity is to live in harmony with nature. My study focused primarily on the Northern Cheyenne tradition because that was the reservation where I had worked and that tribe had the greatest influence on me. As I studied the Medicine Wheel and the animals depicted in each quadrant, I realized that each animal had a valuable lesson to teach that is applicable to both the business world and the field of education. The Medicine Wheel also contains insight into the way humans can achieve more fulfilling lives by adhering to the habits and inclinations of nature's two- and four-footed creatures.

In addition to the Northern Cheyenne tradition, I relied on the Lakota Sioux tradition in identifying the Medicine Wheel's spiritual, emotional, physical, and mental energies. Each one is vital to the balance of your journey.

For those with no prior knowledge of the Medicine Wheel or very little, this book will serve as an introduction. If you already have knowledge of the Medicine Wheel, you may gain a different perspective or see a facet of the Medicine Wheel that you have never experienced before.

Thank you for choosing to read this book. It is my hope that it brings you closer to nature with a newfound appreciation for Native American spirituality and opens your life to a new way of thinking and relating to others. Good luck on your journey!

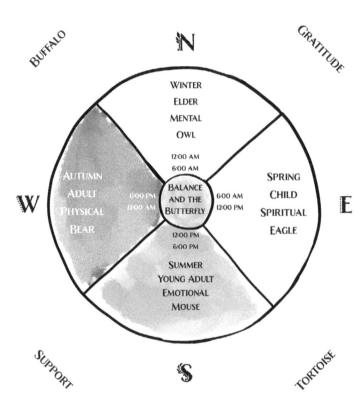

YOUR INVITATION TO THE MEDICINE WHEEL

The Medicine Wheel is an archetype, meaning that it is a pattern repeated over and over again in nature. As the name implies, the Medicine Wheel is a journey — a journey as personal and unique as each individual who dares to take the next step. Many of us have already embarked on the journey and given it different names: path, pilgrimage, road to recovery, climbing the corporate ladder. Even Dorothy had her yellow brick road. While everyone is seeking to find their way, the Medicine Wheel teaches how to walk the path the way nature intended — in cycles. A dark period in one's life may seem like never-ending torment, only to be followed by a flood of light. It's nature's way. One must go through a period of darkness, a time of isolation, in some cases depression or anxiety, before experiencing the dawn of light. Does the little tiny seed that is placed in the ground say,

"What did I do to deserve this?" Sometimes we have to die, "be buried," in order to live our life to its fullest potential. The deep, dark wintertime of our lives eventually leads to springtime; a time of budding and sprouting that will eventually lead to summer; a time of productivity only to be followed by autumn; a time of harvest to be followed again by a time of darkness and silence. And then the cycle begins again. Knowing where you are in your cycle and what comes next helps you make the right choices, avoid future problems, and tap into the resources that nature has to offer.

Before you even begin to read this book, go for a nature walk. Don't go for a strenuous hike to test your physical endurance. Go for a real nature walk where your goal is to attune yourself with every animal, insect, plant, or mineral that crosses your path. Go for at least an hour and go alone. This is your own personal journey and your own unique connection with nature. If you take someone with you, you will get caught up in the conversation.

Don't take your cell phone with you either. These are all distractions and you want to get away from all that, at least for an hour or so. And don't even think of bringing your thoughts from school or work with you. Everything you left behind will be there when you get back.

The time of day you choose to go for your walk is important. Time plays an important part in nature and you will see, hear, and notice different things depending on the time of day or night that you choose to take your nature walk.

Where you choose to walk is also important. Try to get as close to nature as possible: the beach, the woods, the desert. If you live in a big city, force yourself to get away from the concrete jungle and find a special place where you can connect with nature, maybe a park or a nearby pond.

As you walk, take in the physical beauty around you. Notice the trees, the grass, rock formations, animals, mountains, hills, clouds, the sunrise or the sunset, whatever comes within sight and sound. Notice everything from the smallest insect to the highest mountain. And remember to listen. From the first bird chirp in the morning to the nighttime howl of the coyote, the sounds all have messages and meaning. It is your mission to be open, attentive, and intuitive.

As you walk be cognizant of the temperature, time of day, and the season, and ask yourself, "How do I fit into this picture?" "What is my role to play in this grand scheme of Creation?" Hopefully, this book will help you answer that and many other daunting questions concerning the direction of your life.

All of nature is a dynamic array of perfectly aligned plants, trees, shrubs, flowers, insects, and animals working together and you are a part of that group dynamic. Once you connect with nature, the Creator will help you define who you are and what you were meant to do. At first things might be hazy, not in full focus, but the dawn's light will allow you to "see" what is coming up on the horizon. Slowly, gradually, things will come into focus and you will know exactly what direction to move in. New concepts will be awakened and your life's goals will be set into motion.

The one thing that all of nature has in common from the smallest sea turtle to the largest blue whale, from the tiniest ant to the largest buffalo, is that everything in nature moves. It is a sign of growth. You might ask, "Do mountains move?" Yes, they do. Magnetic movements beneath them cause them to move vertically, forming new mountains. They also move along with the continents that are resting on tectonic plates. This is the power of nature and the Medicine Wheel allows you to tap into that power. Nature is always moving and so are you. Your wheel can move fast or slow, depending on your own pace. Metaphorically, your wheel will take you over bumps, potholes, and patches, but you will also experience a smooth ride, coastal views, and scenic heights. This is why we love roller coasters. They are a mini adventure of what life is — movement up and down, sometimes fast and sometimes slow, but always thrilling and exciting.

While it is natural to be in a constant state of motion, it is important to be moving in the right direction. Right now, determine the four cardinal directions from where you are positioned. What direction are you facing? What direction do you face while at work? What direction do you face as you drive to work? When you drive home? What direction does your house face? What direction do you face while sleeping? What part of the country do you live in? What part of the world do you vacation in? As you journey through your Medicine Wheel take note of the one cardinal direction that seems to play a more prominent role in your life. The quadrant that correlates with that cardinal direction may offer insight into the "direction" your life is meant to take. This book will help you identify the characteristics of each cardinal direction and you will be able to determine which one fits your life's circumstances.

Sometimes you are forced to take a step back and that's okay as long as it eventually helps you to move forward. Are you going in the right direction? Do you know what direction you are headed in? Are you getting closer to your goals? Look back at the past few years. What growth has taken place? Don't think in terms of possessions or material wealth. Think in terms of your spiritual, emotional, physical, and mental health. That's the Lakota way. These are the four energies that you will be analyzing in reference to the Medicine Wheel and how the Medicine Wheel can help you grow in those areas. If you are operating according the laws of nature, your growth will take place exponentially. If you are operating contrary to the laws of nature you will still grow, but you will be not be growing at a very efficient rate.

Growth is sometimes painful. You can be placed in a difficult situation, almost unbearable, but it will ultimately result in your own evolution, your own growth. Something good can spring from even the deepest, darkest moments of despair. It has to happen that way. It is how nature works.

Behind nature is the Creator. The Creator will guide your Medicine Wheel as long as you are cooperating with the laws of nature. As you work with the Creator, the divine plan for your life will begin to unfold. There is something beautiful behind the scenes that waits patiently to come into being and you play a role in making it happen. Are you working in cooperation with nature? Are you working in conjunction with the master plan? If you are, you can move forward with confidence and fearlessness knowing that your actions are in accordance with Creation and you cannot fail.

Now step into the eastern quadrant!

GRANDFATHER SKY

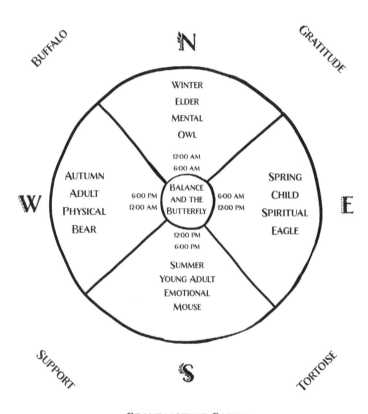

GRANDMOTHER EARTH

CHAPTER ONE
THE EAST AND THE EAGLE

*The eagle flies higher than any other creature,
stretching the dawn across the sky, bringing
illumination to the land below.*

Quadrant: East

Time of Day: 6:00am – 12:00pm

Season: Spring

Stage in Life: Childhood

Emphasis: Spiritual well-being

Animal: Eagle

Color: Golden Yellow

You will begin your Medicine Wheel journey in the east, where the sun comes up. It is the time when the dawn breaks through the darkness and the sky is filled with light extending upwards until the noonday sun. The season is springtime. This time of year announces an array of new beginnings. For this reason, the eastern quadrant represents childhood and all the curiosity that comes with it. Emphasis will be placed on your spiritual state of well-being — your imagination, your creativity, your inner spark. The animal that will help you at this phase of your journey is the eagle. The eagle flies higher than any other creature, stretching the dawn across the sky, bringing illumination to the land below. The eagle will shine light on your path and guide your future. Since this quadrant emphasizes the rising sun, the element is fire; the fire that will ignite your passions. The color is golden yellow. You wear yellow and gold when you want to bring cheer and sunshine to those around you.

The eastern quadrant brings you a greater appreciation of each and every day. As you first awaken, while still in bed, you might map out the day, thinking about how you want your day to unfold. What is first on your agenda? Who do you need to talk with? What do you want to accomplish today? You might set your alarm earlier so you have time to formulate your day before you even get out of bed. Once you get up, you might step outside and personally greet the sun and offer the day up to the Creator. Next you might begin the day with a few morning exercises. Or you might read a meaningful quote to inspire your day. Whatever you choose to do, you always acknowledge the day with an open heart and open arms ready to give and to receive what the Medicine Wheel has to offer. Every day is the chance to start over again, to look for new opportunities, to meet new people, or to gain valuable insight. Your life becomes exciting because you anticipate good things.

Here is where you tap into the energy of the season. What makes seeds sprout? The flowers bloom? The trees grow leaves? The earth's energy has been lying still during the winter season, dormant. Now the forces of nature are awakened and the earth comes alive. What type of seeds are you planting? Are you planting seeds that foster creativity and ingenuity? Are you cultivating a garden of good relationships, both personal and professional? Are you pursuing interests that will make your life bloom with creativity and spark? What you plant today will manifest in the future. It may take years for your ideas to manifest, but it will happen. It's nature's law.

SPRING, THE TIME FOR YOUTHFUL JOY AND CHILDLIKE CURIOSITY

Because it is springtime, it is the time for youthful joy and childlike curiosity. No matter what your chronological age, you are always young at heart. Your curiosity does not diminish with age. As long as you remain interested in life, your curiosity will only increase, leading you down different paths as you take up activities that you never even dreamed of before. Follow that childlike curiosity and see where it takes you.

This will cause you to experience a strong sense of well-being inside. This quadrant represents the spiritual dimension of your Medicine Wheel journey, which is manifested by the spirit that resides in you — the fire that can't be extinguished, the light that won't go out, the force that keeps on burning. Remember the element associated with this quadrant is fire and the fire inside of you ignites all of your plans. Your joy, your enthusiasm, your passion creates a warmth and a glow that attracts people to you. These are the right kind of people; people like you who are smart, creative, and talented. They will help you reach your goals.

READY FOR TAKEOFF

The animal associated with the east is the eagle. The eagle carries the dawn across the sky, extinguishing the dark and spreading the light. The eagle glides forward and upward beyond the horizon, relying on the warm currents beneath its wings. You too will soar like the eagle, but first you have to get out of the nest. You have been in the cozy, warm, comfortable nest for a while; now you want to feel the thrill of taking flight. You are no longer satisfied with watching others soar above you. You want to experience the feeling of euphoria for yourself.

At first you stand on the rim of the nest, looking down at the distance below and then looking upward toward the limitless sky. You gallantly spread your wings. They go beyond the width of the nest. You have no idea of the potential that resides in you. You gaze up at the sky, flap your wings, and begin to take flight. It is a little bit scary at first, but as soon as you take off you feel the warm current beneath you and it is galvanizing. Now you will begin to rely on the invisible forces of nature. Power that you never knew existed fills your entire being.

At first you stay close to the nest, but as your confidence builds you go higher and higher. Each time you leave the nest you go further and further beyond your wildest expectations. The wind carries you to wherever you want to go. The view is spectacular. Suddenly, you can see all that nature has in store for you. It is astounding. As you travel across the sky, you see all the possibilities that lie ahead of you. You feel incredibly strong and you have a strong sense of exhilaration. You don't just understand aerodynamics, you experience it.

Something really special happens as you take flight. All the rejection that you ever experienced is now the force that lifts you higher. All the hurts, attacks, insults, unjust criticisms that were so devastating, now work to your advantage. All the negativity that came in your direction, nature uses it to lift you up. It is an amazing feeling and difficult to fully grasp that something that once kept you down is now the very thing that lifts you up. Nature has done that for you. Nature has turned the forces of negativity into a power that allows you to glide through life, unfettered and free. Now the eagle carries you far away from the people who sought to destroy you. They are only a memory, a very distant memory as the forces of nature carry you across the sky to something beyond your wildest imagination.

You begin to understand that the years of rejection were a necessary part of your flight preparation. You needed to build endurance and resilience, and the rejections you suffered helped you define who you truly are and where you want to go. As you soar above the clouds, the insults and negative criticisms that once caused great pain and sorrow can't touch you. That burden has been lifted from you. As a result you fly higher than you ever thought possible. Nothing can hold you down. You no longer are held captive to someone else's arbitrary set of rules and regulations that had nothing to do with your own personal goals and beliefs. You are free. You are in partnership with nature and your own true nature has nothing to do with painful emotions. Since you are free of someone else's idea of what you should be, you ironically place higher demands on yourself than anyone else ever could because you know your true potential and you fly towards it. You set your own goals, chart your own course, and search for your true meaning. The eagle teaches you to go as far and as high as you can until something in the not so far off distance captures your attention.

And then the miracle happens. You catch a sudden glimpse of your future. In a flash of light, you know what you are meant to do. It isn't someone else's dream for you. It isn't society's expectations of you. It isn't following in someone else's footsteps. It is your own unique idea of who you are and what you want to become. You have so much to give to the world, you will burst onto the scene with fire and intensity, even if no one notices or cares about who you are or what you do.

It doesn't matter. You don't have to answer to anyone. You are your own person and you only answer to yourself and the Creator. This is your personal illumination.

Few people achieve this. Most learn to take orders and follow the crowd. They spend their entire lives trying to "fit in." Their lives become dull and boring and they never rise above the monotony. They accept it and become comfortable with it. But you won't settle for that. You can't. You know that there is something greater out there for you to do. Relying on the eagle, you rise above the ordinary, the status quo, the humdrum of life. There will be some who will be jealous of you and even try to copy you, but it won't work. These people are fake and phony, and nature never rewards them. Actually, nature has a consequence for them. You, to the contrary, are always authentic. You stay true to your course and in time you will be rewarded beyond anything you could have ever imagined.

SETBACKS, TIMING

Don't kid yourself. There can be setbacks. You always have to make sure that your timing and your rhythm are in alignment with nature's currents. Are you relying on the winds of the east to allow you to soar to greater heights? Or are you flapping incessantly and barely getting off the ground, burning up energy as you go, finding yourself exhausted and worn out? It might not be time yet for you to take off. This can be frustrating. Timing is so important. All of nature has its own rhythm and pattern and you might not have found that pattern and rhythm for your own life yet. If your ideas are not manifesting like you want them to, your timing may be off. You may have to take a step back and wait it out. Remember, sometimes you have to take a step back in order to move forward. When it's your springtime, nature works with you to make things happen. If you find yourself exerting enormous amounts of energy with little return, you might need to wait. Your waiting period may be a few weeks, a few months, or maybe even a few years, but eventually you will get out of the nest. For now, all you can do is sit patiently for nature to run its course. Exerting yourself against nature will only bring frustration and heartache.

Maybe you're still sitting in the nest fearful of what lies ahead, or unsure of your own potential. Get up, stand up on the rim of the nest, and spread your wings. This is your time to take flight and let your dreams soar. Are you able to fly fearlessly and gracefully as far and as high as possible? From that perspective, can you see the big picture? Can you see it unfold in front of you? How far up can you fly without losing sight of your goals?

No matter how high you fly, remember to keep your feelings in check. You might get too excited and lose sight of what you want to accomplish. You are on the verge of something really great in your life and it is important to remain focused and steady. Keep the rhythms and the patterns of your flight in alignment with nature. Nature will never have you fly too high or give you too hard a landing.

Now, don't take it literally. You don't have to quit your job and spend a month on a mountain-top meditating on the horizon. It would be nice if you could do that, but that is not really necessary. The lesson of the eagle is to fly above your situation and look at it from a different perspective. When you are stuck in a rut or too comfortable with your situation, it becomes necessary to take flight and see what else the world has to offer. That is what it means to get out of the nest. Once you take flight, you set your sights above the horizon to determine what you really want to do with your life and where you want to go. Think of something grand that only you can do, then set your heart on achieving it.

YOUR MISSION STATEMENT

In practical terms, the eagle helps you identify your life's mission. Now that you have taken flight and caught a glimpse of what you want to accomplish and have landed firmly in reality, this is a good time to write down a mission statement. It's one thing to have an abstract idea of what you want to do; it's another thing when you actually sit down and articulate what it is that you want to achieve. It may take days, weeks, even months for you to compose your very own personal mission statement, but it's worth the effort. It doesn't have to be a book. A few sentences or paragraphs will do. You may want to post it or even frame it and hang it in a prominent place in your home. It will serve as a constant reminder of what you are trying to do and it will keep you on track.

In addition to writing your mission statement, you can establish a habit of writing down your goals. These may be daily, weekly, and yearly goals. They will keep you on track and focused on what you want to accomplish. The eagle has taken you to new heights, so you are bold in creating lofty goals.

The next step is to find a company, corporation, non-profit, or small business that matches your personal mission statement. Most people go off to work, day in and day out, totally unaware of their company's mission statement. If that is you, right now go to your company's website and find their mission statement. Does the company's mission match up with yours? You don't have to quit your job and start sending out resumes if it doesn't. You were attracted to your company for a reason and you were hired for a reason, so you already have a connection. In an ideal situation your company's mission will complement your own. It's a reciprocal relationship. Your company's mission statement helps you grow as an individual while your personal mission statement contributes to the good of the company. Some of you will eventually leave the company, as the eagle leaves its nest, and establish your own company, non-profit, or small business, but until that time, make sure your personal mission statement matches the mission statement of your place of employment. Otherwise it will be miserable for you and those around you.

As high as the eagle flies, it still has to land. No matter how high your sights take you, you still need to remain grounded in reality. Once you have landed, you can begin to lay down the groundwork for what it is that you want to manifest in your life. Remember, the element of the east is fire, and you use that fire to ignite your dreams and goals and make them a reality.

SUMMER SOLSTICE TRANSITION

In the eastern quadrant you have learned to soar, and in the process, you caught a glimpse of your life's purpose. You have written your own personal mission statement. Now you are ready to embark on the most productive season of your life. It's summertime! But first you will make a transition. This is your summer solstice; the longest day in the year when the sun appears to be at its highest point in the sky. Remember that your seasons may last for years. When you are entering your summer season, your solstice will be characterized by an intense energy and a burst of emotion. Something will happen to let you know that you are transitioning from the east to the south. It could be an unexpected promotion or job opportunity — a jolt that catapults you into the next quadrant. Or, it may be a small, subtle change, hardly noticeable, but something will happen to cause you to transition to the next quadrant.

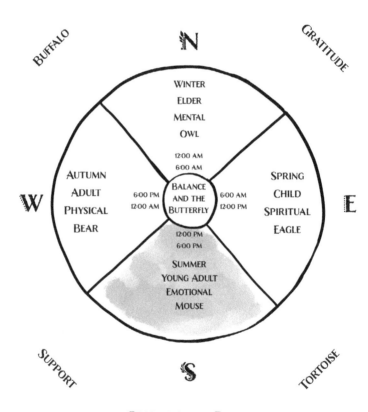

GRANDFATHER SKY

GRATITUDE

BUFFALO

N

WINTER
ELDER
MENTAL
OWL

12:00 AM
6:00 AM

AUTUMN
ADULT
PHYSICAL
BEAR

W

6:00 PM
12:00 AM

BALANCE
AND THE
BUTTERFLY

6:00 AM
12:00 PM

SPRING
CHILD
SPIRITUAL
EAGLE

E

12:00 PM
6:00 PM

SUMMER
YOUNG ADULT
EMOTIONAL
MOUSE

SUPPORT

S

TORTOISE

GRANDMOTHER EARTH

CHAPTER TWO
THE SOUTH AND THE MOUSE

The mouse teaches you self-discipline, as well as organizational and social skill sets. The mouse also teaches you to trust in yourself.

Quadrant: South

Time of Day: 12:00pm – 6:00pm

Season: Summer

Stage in Life: Young Adult

Emphasis: Emotional well-being

Animal: Mouse

Color: Red

As you move into the southern quadrant you will experience intense activity. The time of day stretches from the noonday sun till the sun sets in the horizon. The season is summer. The southern quadrant represents young adulthood and major life decisions. In this quadrant emphasis will be placed on your emotional well-being. The animal that helps you achieve your goals at this stage of your Medicine Wheel journey is the mouse. The mouse teaches you self-discipline, as well as organizational and social skill sets. You will learn to pay attention to details. The mouse also teaches you to trust in yourself. The element for this quadrant is water and you will need it since your garden is in full bloom. The color is red symbolizing intensity, but also caution. You wear red when you want to make a bold statement.

This is the time when the sun is the brightest and the most intense, and so goes your life. During this time energy and spontaneity infuse every cell of your body. Optimism and zest are your constant companions. Your days are long and filled with incredible productivity and efficiency. You are able to coordinate several activities in a single day and you are able to achieve more than you set out to do. You come home at night with a tremendous sense of accomplishment that only fuels you up for the next day.

SUMMER, THE TIME FOR GROWTH, PRODUCTIVITY, AND FUN

This is your summertime and your schedule is packed. Because you are in alignment with nature, everything works like clockwork. Your timing is impeccable. You never miss a beat. Everything goes exactly the way you planned. Your life has never been so good. Nothing can stop you. You are unbeatable. You are amazed at all that you can accomplish. No matter how much work comes at you, you are able to take it on. You thrive in this environment.

This quadrant represents young adulthood. Whether pursuing a college degree, choosing a career, building a business, or growing a family, this is the time when you will experience tremendous growth and development. For that reason you are very careful with the decisions you make. At the time of your decision-making, you make what you think is the best choice under the present circumstances. While you have the freedom to choose your own way, you will eventually reap the consequences of your choices whether right or wrong. In some cases the wrong choice is the only way for you to learn. Eventually, you will learn to live a peaceful and harmonious life based on one simple principle — every decision you make will come back to you. It might take years for the effects of your decisions to manifest, but they will manifest in due season.

As the eastern quadrant helped you ignite your spiritual fire, the southern quadrant will help you develop a healthy emotional state of being. Your vibrant personality reaches out to people like the spokes of the Medicine Wheel. You begin to attract people and circumstances that line up with what you want to accomplish. People respond to your energy and are ready to help with your projects.

The animal associated with this quadrant is the mouse. The mouse will help you with your day-to-day activities. Mice are very practical and this is particularly helpful for this phase of your Medicine Wheel. You spent the last quadrant soaring sky high. Now is the time to get down to basics. The mouse teaches you to deal with the present moment and to pay attention to details. You pay attention to every single detail because you know that in the details, mistakes are made. Unlike the eagle who teaches you to see the big picture, the mouse teaches you to concentrate and focus on what is directly in front of you.

You start by organizing your surroundings. Your desk, your office, your house, your car, everything within your immediate vicinity is organized, down to the very last pencil. You know where everything is and this gives you a feeling of security. This habit eliminates worry and anxiety. When you wake up in the morning, you make your bed. When you finish eating, you wash the dishes. Every night before you leave the office, you organize your desk so that when you return the next morning you hit the ground running. You are always striving for ways to make your life more secure and easier to handle. By creating a structured environment for yourself you are in sync with the structures and patterns of nature.

Next, you devise a system that is efficient and practical for everyday needs. You learn to prioritize. You decide what is most important and you tackle that first, then you go down your "to do" list. You check things off as each task is completed. Whatever you didn't finish, you carry over to the next day. This way, things don't fall through the cracks. You keep excellent records. Nothing is haphazard. This is a lifelong process that is achieved through daily habits and it never stops.

The mouse also teaches you to organize your time, primarily by not wasting it. You don't spend mindless hours involved in activities that offer no return. Time, like money, is an investment. You invest wisely. You spend your time doing things that are worthwhile and will bring back huge returns. You establish a rhythm that allows you to work faster and more efficiently.

As you organize your external environment you will begin to notice over time the effect that this habit has on the way you think. Your mind will become clearer and as a result your awareness is sharpened, your productivity increases, and your goals are met. Because you are organized mentally, you get the job done quicker and the faster you work, the more work you get done. You are able to take on twice as many projects as before and you accomplish them in a shorter period of time. You are on top of things, which makes you valuable to your family, your organization, and your community, but most importantly to yourself.

Remember, in this quadrant the emphasis is on your emotional well-being. Because you are organized, your life will become fuller and more satisfying, and that brings you more joy and happiness.

Mice are also quite athletic. They are great climbers and swimmers and they make excellent jumpers. You, too, are climbing in social circles and making huge jumps in your career, business, and in your community. You learn from the mouse how to interact and mingle with those around you.

You learn how to network. It is easy for you to strike up a conversation with just about anyone. You ask questions and you give people your full attention and that is why people like you. You make people feel important because they *are* important. It is summertime and your life is in full swing. Soon you will find yourself being invited to parties, fundraising events, community activities, and other social gatherings. It is here that you learn to network and build relationships that will last a lifetime. Like the mouse you take full advantage of every opportunity for good food and good company. And when you do get invited to the fancy high-profile banquet, you take a hint from the mouse and nibble; you don't gorge yourself. You are trying to make a good impression, not stock up on food!

ALWAYS BE ON ALERT

This can also be a very dangerous time for you, but like the mouse, you are always on alert. You pay attention to what is going on around you. You never want to be caught off guard. You never want to get caught in a trap. The mouse teaches you to be resourceful and diligent, so you are never taken by surprise. Knowing that they are easy prey for cats, birds, and snakes, mice possess an incredible sense of both hearing and smell that keeps them on high alert. You are the same.

Now that you have reached your goals and are riding high, know that this will incur the jealousy of many of those around you. Your uncanny ability to get things done and make things happen will only highlight the fact that they lag behind in ingenuity, creativity, and productivity. The more you accomplish, the more they will seethe with envy. You will see it in their faces. You will hear it in their voices. You will smell something isn't right.

Look to the mouse for help and guidance in this type of situation. Mice are astute in building intricate paths and burrows for shelter and protection. They have survived for millennia by engineering underground escape routes. You too need an escape route, just in case. If someone close to you concocts a plan to hurt, interfere, or sabotage what you are doing, it will only take you to the next level. Bring it on. Be like the little mouse. Devise a plan where you can find a refuge and be safe. Your plans will still go according to nature. Burrow into an escape hatch, come out the other side. The sun will be shining on you. Your adversaries will be left in the dust scrounging around for their next meal, but it won't be you.

When someone criticizes your work, you don't fight back. When someone cuts you down, like plants that are pruned, you will only grow back stronger and greener. It's nature's way. The Medicine Wheel will take care of you and your adversaries. They are not at your level. They are living in their own world, not in relation to the Creator, and therefore they meet with obstacles because they are not in sync with the laws of nature. That is where their frustration comes from and they take it out on you. Ignore them. They are not worthy of your energy, passion, or even a response. Always remember, your emotional well-being is more important than anyone else's opinion of you. Don't go to their level. If you do, your Medicine Wheel will get stuck. Move away from them. The mouse will help you do this. The mouse will teach you to trust in yourself and your own abilities to get out of a difficult situation.

Listen to those around you. Do you smell something in the air? Is it an off the cuff comment that someone made? Do you sense an enemy close to you? Like the little mouse, burrow in tunnels that can keep you safe. They can also lead you to new possibilities. Maybe it's time to take a drastic turn and do something new with your life. Look for unexpected opportunities. Trust that nature has a perfect plan for you. That toxic situation might be just the thing to take you to the next level.

This is a good time to take stock of your true-blue friends. The ones who walked with you during your most difficult moments are the ones you want to keep around you. This is good to know because during the summer when you are in full swing there will be plenty of sunshine friends who will want to attach onto your success. A word of caution here. Be careful of the moochers. These are the takers. They have nothing to offer you; they are only interested in how you can help them, with no concern for you whatsoever. These people can be hard to spot at first. They appear to be very charming. That's part of the manipulation. They are incredibly deceitful. They will show up unexpectedly — out of the blue — and pretend it was by accident, then offer to take you out to dinner or to the movies. And you will think 'what a wonderful surprise!' A week later they will call you and ask you for something that will only benefit them. And then you know that it was a planned attack. One of the best examples is when someone out of your distant past shows up and all of a sudden wants to be your best friend and then you find out that all they really want to do is mooch off you. Stay away from those people. These people are worse than enemies because they pretend to be your friend when all they want is something for themselves. You might have a few interactions with people like this, but it will just make you better equipped to identify them in the future and know how to avoid them. Just as a mouse can smell a cat, the mouse will teach you how to avoid these people.

BE MINDFUL OF WATER

While you are very productive in the southern quadrant, the season can be intense and for that reason nature provides you with a helper. Water plays an important role during all the seasons, but particularly in the summer months. The seeds that you planted months or even years ago have taken root, budded, and are now in full bloom, but your garden still needs water. This is the time in your Medicine Wheel where you will see the most growth take place, so always remember to water your garden. The garden analogy reflects your own personal and professional growth. Make sure to surround yourself with people who nurture and "water" your creativity and your passions.

Always be mindful of water. Make water your friend. Did you ever wonder why so many ideas come to you in the shower? It's a conductor of ideas. And you don't just limit yourself to taking showers — you go to the beach, you swim in the pool, you sing in the rain. You look forward to washing the dishes. Maybe standing at the kitchen sink washing pots and pans will be where you get your greatest inspiration. Ideas will come to you continually throughout your journey on the Medicine Wheel. Be open to them, especially when you are working with water.

Water reminds you to cleanse and purify. This can be done physically, emotionally, spiritually, and mentally. Every day, water will help you take time to refresh, rejuvenate, and let go of any impurities or defilement that can hold you back. And lastly, don't forget to drink it!

But water can also pose a threat to your wheel. What is your relationship with water? Are you riding the big wave? Are you swimming with the current? Are you floating? Are you diving into the deep end? Are you drowning? Are you being tossed out to sea? If you feel as if water is working against you, the timing might not be right, you might have to take a step back and wait it out, just like in the eastern quadrant. Nature doesn't work on your clock, you work with nature's clock. So, take a few steps back and relax in the sand. Wait for the surf to come in and then ride the wave for as long and as far as you can.

AUTUMN EQUINOX TRANSITION

In the eastern quadrant, you were able to visualize your future and articulate your very own mission statement. In the southern quadrant you developed impeccable organizational skills, uncanny survival skills, and extraordinary networking skills. Now you are ready to enter the western quadrant, but first there will be a shift to announce that you are entering into another phase of your Medicine Wheel. This is your autumn equinox. Like the summer solstice that you experienced earlier, something will happen to let you know you are entering into the next phase of your Medicine Wheel. It can be a drastic transition or a subtle passage. Be on alert. This is not something that you will do. It is something that nature will give you, almost like a reward for your good work and staying on your true course. It might be a bonus, a get-away vacation, an unexpected yet delightful change in plans. Be on the lookout. Then you will enter the western quadrant.

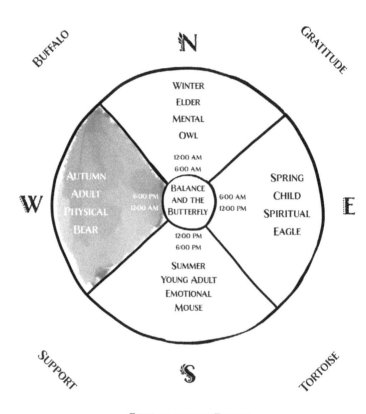

CHAPTER THREE
THE WEST AND THE BEAR

Bears are great communicators. They clack their teeth, snort, whine, grunt, and moan. Bears also teach the importance of introspection and self-evaluation.

Quadrant: West

Time of Day: 6:00pm – 12:00am

Season: Autumn

Stage of Life: Adult

Emphasis: Physical well-being

Animal: Bear

Color: Black

The western quadrant represents the time from dusk to midnight. Things begin to slow down and cool down. It is the end of the day. It is the autumn time of year, the time of harvest. It is also the time for "letting go" and "cutting loose." The element of obsidian helps you to do this. In the lifetime cycle, this quadrant represents the adult years. In this quadrant emphasis will be placed on your physical well-being. The animal that helps you at this stage of your Medicine Wheel journey is the bear. The bear teaches you how to communicate effectively. The bear also teaches you the importance of reflection and introspection. The color of this quadrant is black, symbolizing victory. You wear black when you want to show respect and dignity.

This is the time of day when work is over. You clear things off your desk and call it a day; but before you go, you assess what you accomplished and you set your goals for the next day. Then you leave it all behind and head home. Now you can let your mind relax and do something that brings balance to your workday. Watch a movie, take your spouse out to dinner, go play with your kids or your pet animals. Or just find a quiet spot, park the car and watch the sunset. This is a vital part of your day. If you don't take time to relax now, you will drag tomorrow. Whatever was at the forefront of your thinking, let it sit on the back burner. Let your subconscious mind work on it and you will be amazed at what comes forth the next day. This is an important part of productivity. The sunset reminds you to set your work aside on a daily basis.

AUTUMN, THE TIME FOR LETTING GO AND CUTTING LOOSE

This is your autumn, a time for letting go. Just as leaves fall from the trees and are whisked away, you too practice the art of "letting go." You might want to clean out a closet, a room, or a garage. Once you do this, you will notice how the energy flow around you changes. Things and events you are involved with move smoothly and effortlessly because you have cleared the energy channels around you and your physical world is in sync with nature. Or you might do the inner work of letting go of a deep-seated resentment from something that happened a long time ago. It's buried so deep down, you might not even be conscious of it, but it's still there and at some point, you will have to deal with it. Now is the time to let go of all the events, emotions, and memories that are holding you back. Once you are able to shake the negativity, your energy flow is unobstructed. Your mind is literally unfettered and able to grasp complex ideas and concepts that will move you forward. This is all because you are able to "let go." You create a void for something greater and more powerful to enter.

Even more powerful than letting go, you may have to cut something or someone loose. Is there some "thing" in your life that is holding you back, not allowing you to move forward? Is there someone in your life who is causing hardship or heartache? Are you holding on to that person out of fear of being alone? Are you holding on for security reasons? Are you holding on for lack of self-esteem? None of these emotions help you on your Medicine Wheel journey. As difficult as it may be, you might have to cut that thing or person out of your life. The act of cutting is a little stronger than letting go, since you have to exert more energy than the person or thing that is holding on to you. You have to purposely force someone or something out of your life. It may be painful, but necessary if your Medicine Wheel is to move forward. In a true and lasting friendship, both persons make sacrifices, but both persons benefit from the relationship as well. If you are in a relationship where the other person is sucking the life out of you — sucking you dry emotionally, physically, mentally, spiritually, even financially — you need to get rid of that person. You need to cut them loose, the sooner the better. Nature has provided you with a tool to help you do this —

obsidian. Still used today as a surgical tool, obsidian is the sharpest cutting edge there is. It is a small stone, but it can have a very powerful effect. You can wear the stone around your neck, or keep it close by, on your desk or in a drawer as a reminder of the need to cut some things loose, even people. Be strong. If you are in a relationship that is holding you back from your full potential, get rid of that person.

THE HARVEST

This quadrant represents adulthood where you reap the benefits of all your good thoughts, good decisions, and good actions that you manifested throughout the last two quadrants. The garden you planted in the spring is ready for harvest. A feeling of abundance will take place in your life. It isn't necessarily material wealth, although it could be. More importantly, you may experience strong family ties and solid friendships. In your business dealings, you have treated people fairly and justly. As a result, honest and trustworthy people want to do business with you. You have a feeling of security and confidence in knowing that things are going your way. And for this you are grateful. You have worked hard for sure, but nature has given you the tools to work with — guidance from the animals, seasonal changes, and the wisdom of the elements. Driven by your tremendous sense of gratitude, you share your abundance with others.

This quadrant represents your physical well-being. You take a three-pronged approach: exercise, proper nutrition, and sleep. You set aside three or four times a week for exercise. You find an exercise activity that you truly love and then stick with it. It shouldn't be something that you dread. It should be something that you look forward to doing. Splurge on that bike you have been thinking about getting. Go ahead and get that trampoline. Go ice-skating on a Sunday afternoon. Physical recreation is meant to be fun, not a chore. Once you adopt an exercise program, you will want to eat right. You will want to eat fresh fruits and vegetables. You will want to make yourself a fruit smoothie in the morning. You will want a salad with dinner. Physical exercise and nutrition really do go together. Lastly, don't forget to allow yourself enough time to sleep. There's nothing worse than someone saying, "you look tired." So make sure that you get to bed at a decent time.

THE ART OF COMMUNICATION

The animal that guides you in the autumn season is the bear. Bears are great communicators. They clack their teeth, snort, whine, grunt, and moan. They also scratch trees and leave paw markings on their territory. The bear teaches you how to communicate effectively. In some cases, you will be very nurturing and kind. At other times, you will have to use tact and diplomacy. In other instances, you will have to be stern and unrelenting. The bear teaches you how to do all that and then some.

How effectively do you communicate with others? Does your conversation inspire and motivate others? What words do you use? How extensive is your vocabulary? What tone of voice do you use? Are your words persuasive or do your words merely demonstrate your opinion with no regard for someone else's? Is your voice shrill and obnoxious or is your voice soothing and easy to listen to? Do people respond positively to what you are saying? What messages do you send with your body? What messages do you send with the clothes you wear? Do you communicate with facial expressions?

In this day and age of social media, there are a multitude of ways to communicate with the masses. Are you using these tools effectively? Are you taking full advantage of all that is available to you? Are your emails and text messages appropriate? Are your voice messages long and rambling or to the point? Whatever method of communication you use, you choose your words wisely and people respond to you positively.

EFFECTIVE TOOLS FOR BUSINESS

The western quadrant holds the key to success in business because in this quadrant you acquire the effective tools to motivate your workforce. The bear helps you to do this in a variety of ways; each one of these ways is useful if correctly applied to the situation at hand. Each situation has its own unique circumstances, and the bear helps you identify the issue and apply the right strategy for success.

Because of your ability to communicate effectively and persuasively, people seek you out. They want to know what you have to say. When you speak, you speak truthfully and candidly. By interacting with people in this manner, you gain their respect and admiration. You acquire a sterling reputation that never tarnishes because when you speak, you speak the truth. In speaking the truth, you use as few words as possible and you avoid saying anything negative about another person. Gossip is never a part of your speech. Whenever you are in a situation where gossip is taking over, you quickly make an exit. Gossip is toxic and weighs you down. You take no part in it.

As a master communicator, you know that listening is just as important as speaking. When you listen to someone you give them your full attention. Those who think they can multi-task while someone is speaking to them are fooling themselves. If you engage in another activity while someone is talking to you, you are sending a strong message that what the other person is saying is not important. This is unprofessional, inappropriate, and just plain ignorant. When someone is speaking to you, you stop what you are doing; you look them in the eye and let them finish before you respond. Even if it is a child, you never interrupt. You learned self-discipline in the last quadrant, so this will be easy for you.

You never show favoritism. Favoritism is a deviation of the truth and truth is the standard you operate under. Your thoughts, words, and actions always reflect the truth. Favoritism twists the truth. It turns a blind eye. You never play favorites, because playing favorites is a weakness and no one will respect you for it. It is okay to work with your friends as long as you can draw the line between professional and personal. Like the bear, you know how to take a stand. You never put your friendship above the mission of the organization you are working for. It breeds corruption and leads to a dysfunctional workplace. People who have skills and talent will leave because they know friendships will be rewarded and not their job performance. This leads ultimately to a collapse in the organization. But you don't operate that way. You treat everyone fairly and your people love you for it. They won't say it publicly, but they love you for treating them the way they should be treated and they will always remain loyal to you.

You also communicate effectively when you are called upon to evaluate someone else's work. Evaluations are a very effective method of communication. When they are done wisely they can be very powerful. When evaluations are used properly and in a professional manner people want them. Evaluations in the hands of someone who doesn't know what they are doing can be destructive and hurtful. Just as the bear has incredible capacity for destruction, poor and misguided evaluations result in misunderstanding, a breakdown in communication, and poor morale. You avoid that because you know the right way to evaluate a person or situation. You evaluate a person's job performance with respect and dignity, not condescension. You are positive in your assessment and you help the person grow.

You don't use evaluations to get rid of someone because you know that is wrong. Maybe someone has done that to you in the past and you have experienced first-hand that kind of injustice, so you make every effort to not let that happen to anyone who works for you. Just as an interaction with a bear can be a deadly confrontation, so too can an evaluation that is not done properly. People who use an evaluation as a weapon are deadly, even to themselves. They operate in fear. They see others who are doing a better job than they are and they feel threatened, so they react the only way they know how. They undermine someone else's work to protect their own position. They might succeed in getting rid of the person, but the problem still remains. They are dealing with insecurity issues that will grow and stifle their own abilities. It takes years to reverse this and they are setting themselves up for ultimate failure. But you don't operate that way. You don't have fear. You possess only understanding and patience for those around you. You understand the journey and the difficulties, so you skillfully make the journey lighter. As a result, the difficulties disappear.

When you are called to write an evaluation, you do it positively and professionally. People look forward to your comments about the job they are doing. Most people go to work and try to do a good job and you recognize their sincere desire to do good work. You acknowledge all the positive things he or she is doing. You point out the direction you want them to go in. If the person is moving in the wrong direction you make them aware of it, but not with animosity or hostility. You use diplomacy and tact in helping your employees grow in the same direction as the company. Instead of feeling downtrodden and rejected, they walk out of your office actually feeling good about themselves because now they know what areas they need to concentrate on and how to become better at what they do. Everyone wants to improve, so you have done them a huge favor. Instead of walking out of your office like a dog that has just been beaten, your employee walks out of your office empowered and motivated to do a better job. You never gain anything by criticizing someone in the wrong way. It takes a truly diplomatic person to evaluate a person's job performance in a way that makes them feel better about themselves, not worse. Very few people have mastered those skills, but you're a crackerjack. You have just set into motion a powerful action: employees feel good about themselves. In turn they will do a better job, increase production, and grow with the company. You have created your own microcosm of nature. You are in charge of your own little ecosystem and everyone is working to his or her maximum potential.

THE BENEFITS OF INTROSPECTION

Now that you have mastered the art of evaluating others, it is time for introspection and self-evaluation. The bear helps you to do this as well. Just as the bear slows down during the autumn season and prepares for hibernation by retreating into his den, you too create your own den, your own inner sanctuary. As you spend time in your den you reflect and look back over your Medicine Wheel to assess what you have learned and how you have grown. You look over the past few months or years and reflect on what you have created. What came out of nothing? What could you have done differently? What have you learned from your Medicine Wheel journey? How have you helped other people on their journey? Did you achieve all that you set out to do or did you go beyond what you had initially set out to accomplish? What fell through the cracks? As for the things that didn't get done, are they worth pursuing or do you want to channel your energy in a different direction? Keep track of your achievements. They will give you a sense of accomplishment and a foundation to build on.

Or, you might look back and think to yourself, 'I did it all wrong. I am at a point in my life where I want to go back and change everything that I did because I got it all wrong.' Or, you might look back on that one major blunder that changed the direction of your life forever; you wish that you could go back and change it, but you can't. Focusing your thoughts on past mistakes will take you away from your true purpose. All your failures, wrong turns, mistakes — all your 'would have, should have, could haves,' all your 'if only I had done it this way' or 'if only I hadn't done it this way' — were all an important part of your life's fabric. You will have regrets, certainly. Anyone who says they don't have regrets hasn't lived. Your regrets tell you that you have learned something and you are a better person than before. Your failures are part of your journey. Accept them as that. Go beyond your mistakes. Don't wallow in them or hold on to them. Be grateful for them and then discipline yourself to look forward. Once you have accepted your mistakes and moved beyond them, nature does something truly incredible and turns your mistakes into something positive. Your mistakes will be part of your transformation. Nature does this and you will be amazed to see how something so wrong can turn into something so right.

What you thought were your biggest mistakes can actually be used to your greatest advantage. You get creative. You use them as reminders of what not to do. You use them, but don't let them hang over you like a dark cloud that follows you around no matter where you go. You look for the lesson in the mistake and you use it for something good. As bad as your past may be, take the future and make it eclipse your past. Conquer your past by emboldening your future. No matter what your past is, at this point in your Medicine Wheel journey you have accepted it and you should experience a strong sense of empowerment that will take your life to the next level.

WINTER SOLSTICE TRANSITION

Your wheel continues to turn as you cross over the winter solstice and you enter the northern quadrant. You will enter into a deep state of sub-consciousness that will fuel your next Medicine Wheel and you will begin to dream of new things to come. As your body sleeps, your subconscious mind will awaken your intuition, your artistic inspiration, and your imagination. But this will happen in the dead of night. That's how nature works. You will also learn the true meaning behind the work that you do. Now you will enter into the northern quadrant, the last quadrant of your Medicine Wheel.

GRANDFATHER SKY

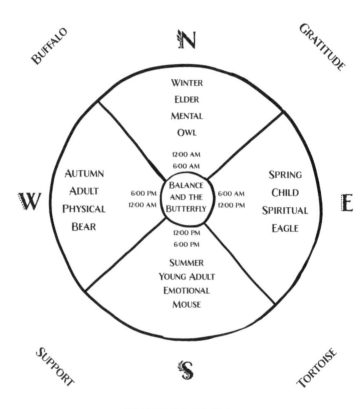

GRANDMOTHER EARTH

CHAPTER FOUR
THE NORTH AND THE OWL

The owl sits patiently and silently, observing and listening to the messages of the night. The owl can see things in the dark and at great distances.

Quadrant: North

Time of Day: 12:00am – 6:00am

Season: Winter

Stage in Life: Elder

Emphasis: Mental well-being, intuition

Animal: Owl

Color: White

The northern quadrant is the time from midnight to dawn when nature is still. It is a time of silence. It is the time to sleep and to dream. The season is winter; a time of isolation, loneliness, and darkness. In terms of the human lifecycle, you have reached elder status. In this quadrant emphasis will be placed on your mental well-being. This is where you develop your intuition, your "knowing." The northern winds and the cold air sharpen your mind and your mental outlook. The animal that helps you during this season is the owl. The color is white, the color of snow. You wear white to symbolize knowledge and wisdom.

As nature begins to wind down and enter into the world of stillness, you too prepare for a good night's sleep. "Getting ready for bed" becomes an important ritual because you know that preparing for sleep places your subconscious mind in a position to tap into nature's resources. Every night as you fall asleep, you awaken to the spirit world of ideas, dreams, and visions. To aid in this process, you create a bedroom that is conducive to a good night's sleep. You eliminate all clutter and unnecessary objects. You might have a picture or two to meditate on as you fall asleep or something positive to look at the moment you open your eyes in the morning.

WINTER, A TIME OF STILLNESS

The northern quadrant symbolizes wintertime when the earth becomes frozen and lifeless. The sky is gray. The landscape becomes bleak and barren. Creatures sleep and trees stand bare. During this season, it appears as though all of nature is dormant, yet deep below the surface the energies of the earth are being awakened. Nature mysteriously sends its energy to all parts of the earth to prepare for the next season of growth. This is what makes the winter season very special, magical in a sense. You don't see what is happening, but something very dramatic is taking place. The garden you planted in the spring lies dormant, yet seeds of spring that lie beneath the surface are being infused with the potential to flower the earth with color, vibrancy, and new life. This quadrant represents your senior years, your "more mature" years. This is the time when things reach their completion. Here, you finish the task you began in the eastern quadrant. You tie up loose ends. Whether it's a month-long project, a yearly enterprise, or a lifetime career, you finish what you started. While many people have grandiose ideas and an unlimited imagination, it is the determined and the diligent who finish what they start. Many people go through life drifting from one project to the next, rarely reaping the benefits of their efforts because they never see their plans through to completion. The northern quadrant of your Medicine Wheel teaches you to finish what you started. This is a time for celebration. You made it completely around the circle!

SEEING IN THE DARK

At this stage in your Medicine Wheel you will develop your intuition and gain knowledge from above. It is important to make the distinction between intuition and conscience. Your conscience dictates what is right or wrong and most people by a certain age can make that distinction, but intuition is different. Your intuition tells you what is best for you. When you have a difficult decision to make between two formidable options, your intuition helps you to make the best choice for you and your circumstances at that time. Once you develop your intuition in smaller decisions, then you can use it to help you to make bigger decisions. Nature has provided you with assistance for developing your intuition — the owl.

The owl sits patiently and silently, observing and listening to the messages of the night. The owl can see things in the dark and at great distances. The owl has the most forward-facing eyes of all birds, yet the owl can rotate its head for a full 360-degree view. They see things that other birds do not have the power to see. You too will experience powerful visions in the night if you practice patience and silence. As you sleep, you dream, and nature provides you with ideas from above — insight, understanding that you can't get during the waking hours. A dream might give you an answer to a problem you have been struggling with. Some of your dreams will reveal something that is about to happen in the immediate future while other dreams will reveal something that will take place decades in the future. You might see a picture or a vision that makes no sense, but in a day, a week, a month, its meaning will become clear. That is why you keep a dream journal. Your dream might not make sense at the time, but sometime in the distant future it will.

The owl is astute in bobbing its head up and down to catch a glimpse of something that may be hidden or obscured. You too become very aware of things around you that others may not notice. You may come across "signs" that will give you direction and guidance. These signs will be very subtle and will only be revealed to you if you are paying attention. You don't ignore these signs, but you test them. If there is any doubt at all in your mind, you hold off. You are not the fool who jumps in at the first "sign" of a good thing. You test the signs and you wait for a confirmation before going forward. There is nothing wrong with that. That is the wisdom the owl brings to you. If you are new at this, you may unknowingly use a sign to forward your own agenda and that will most likely get you into a lot of trouble. However, if you test the signs, then you can move forward with assurance that you are moving in the right direction. You will be glad you paid attention to your intuition and stayed on your true course. On the other hand, if you refuse to follow a sign that was meant specifically for you, your Medicine Wheel will become stuck and your life will go nowhere. Your wheel will take you down a dead-end street. Your life will be meaningless because you did not follow the signs and answer the call.

LISTENING TO THE INNER VOICE; PAYING ATTENTION TO YOUR GUT

The owl also helps you to develop auditory skills. The owl's ears are set to hear the most minute sound. The owl can detect the position of its prey by the slightest rustling of leaves or the movement of foliage. And then it moves in that direction without making a sound. Are you able to sit at night, in the dark and listen quietly? Are you listening before you act? What does your inner voice tell you to do? The inner voice of intuition uses very few words; it is never rambling or incessant. You will hear a voice almost as if a person is speaking inside of you telling you what to do. It may be as simple as "don't take this job" or "get out of here," but it will be firm and unyielding. No matter how contrary your voice is to outside circumstances, you will listen to that voice. It will never do you wrong as long as you test it.

If the voice tells you to sell your house and go to Vegas, you need to test that voice. Is it really your intuition telling you that you are going to get rich in Vegas or is it just wishful thinking?

Your inner voice protects, guides, and instructs. It is always with you as long as you are living in harmony with nature and living a pure life. Your intuition works best when you are in a calm state. The owl teaches you to sit calmly and to be patient. When you are in a state of irritability, anger, or hostility, your inner voice is silenced. Sit in solitude; wait in anticipation. Your voice will come to your aid exactly when you need it. As long as you stay on the right road, your inner voice is clear and audible. If you do go off the path and find yourself at a dead end where your intuition is virtually inaudible, turn around and get back on the straight and narrow road and your inner voice will return.

The owl is a predatory animal, focused and intent, anticipating the kill. It waits patiently, silently, and then attacks at the right moment. It knows when to swoop down and strike its prey. Nature too has provided you with a built-in mechanism that gives you a feeling of "knowing." When making critical decisions, are you able to wait for the right moment or do you rush in without calculating the cost? Can you wait even years to strike at the right time? This is a very valuable skill to have in your repertoire. One wrong move can be costly in terms of time and money. You avoid those mistakes by following your feeling of "knowing." Another name for this is gut reaction.

Your gut reaction can happen spontaneously even with strangers. It isn't a judgement. It isn't discrimination. It's a "knowing." Your gut tells you if the person in front of you is honest or not. Your intuition is operating on peak status because you are living your life based on trustworthiness and integrity. That is why it is so easy for you to pick up on those who are doing the opposite.

Your gut reaction may also be a form of uneasiness. The closer you get to doing something, the more your "gut" feeling will surface. There is a normal anxiety that people experience when they are about to take on a new enterprise, but this is different. This is a strong agitation; your inner self knows something isn't right and it manifests itself with a bad feeling. You almost can't live with yourself if you go forward with the decision. The funny thing is, it might look like the opportunity of a lifetime, but looks are deceiving. Your gut reaction doesn't respond to how something looks, but to how it feels. Even if the world around you is telling you to go in one direction, yet your gut tells you not to, you go with your gut. It takes courage to do this, but if you don't you will regret it. It might take years to recover and you will never forgive yourself for not paying attention to your gut reaction.

As your intuition becomes more precise, greater things will be revealed to you. People

begin to recognize you for your ability to anticipate what will happen in the future. This is a valuable tool that not many people possess. You are
fortunate to have it.

Lastly, your intuition will never lead you to
hurt, harm, or hinder another human being. Your
Medicine Wheel will never lead you down that
path. If you are cheating or stealing or causing any
harm whatsoever, your Medicine Wheel will
come to a complete stop. That is your own selfish
ego that is leading you down the road of destruction and if that is the case, you will need to retrace
your steps and get back on the right road.

MENTORING

Now that you have completed the four quadrants of your Medicine Wheel you have acquired
several skills and learned many lessons. You have
reached elder status and your primary role at this
time is to mentor those who can learn from your
expertise. You have a responsibility to pass on your
knowledge, decision-making skills, communica-

tion mastery, and valuable insight to others so they may achieve their greatest potential. You take someone under your wing. You encourage them by listening to them and supporting their ideas and ambitions. You teach them to be organized and prepared. And you do this by example. You remind them to stay focused when they get distracted. You don't want them to make the same mistakes you made, so when you see them headed in the wrong direction you guide them down a different path. You pass along advice and suggestions. You give compliments when it is appropriate. And they will always come back for more. But you know your boundaries. You never ask questions that are too personal or inappropriate and because of this people are willing to share with you. You are the star mentor.

KEEP MOVING

Even while you are helping other people, your Medicine Wheel is still in motion and that's where the northern winds will push your

Medicine Wheel forward. This will be an incredible force since you will need all that energy to begin your Medicine Wheel all over again. Are you resisting it or are you using that force to your full advantage? It might be a gentle breeze or a 90-mile-an-hour gust of wind. Just know that the winds are moving you in the right direction. Even if the northern winds are taking your Medicine Wheel to a place you don't want to go, you summon up the courage to go where the wind is leading because you know that there is something there for you to do. Remember, nature is on your side; use the forces of nature to help you accomplish your purpose in life.

In the **first quadrant** you defined your purpose and articulated your mission statement.

In the **second quadrant** you developed self-control and set your business in order.

In the **third quadrant** you gained exemplary communication skills and learned how to evaluate effectively, professionally, and personally.

In the **fourth quadrant** you developed your intuition and used your skills and talents to mentor others.

Now you will begin your Medicine Wheel journey all over again...

SPRING EQUINOX TRANSITION

There are many lessons to learn in life so you will experience the Medicine Wheel many times. The owl will help you along your path and will continue to help you. The northern winds are at your back and your Medicine Wheel is moving forward. At this spoke you will move from a period of darkness to a period of light and anticipation. But remember, before you enter into the spring season, something happens. It might be something very subtle or it could be something very grand, but whatever it is, it will propel you forward. This is your spring equinox. The four seasons of your Medicine Wheel along with your equinoxes and solstices will be repeated over and over again throughout your life.

THREE MORE DIMENSIONS

In addition to the four cardinal directions (or quadrants), there are three other dimensions that make your Medicine Wheel turn: center, above, and below. The center balances all the quadrants. Below is represented by the earth. Above is represented by the sky. These dimensions are just as important as the four cardinal directions and they are vital to the movement of your wheel. They too have animal wisdom to help you along your Medicine Wheel journey.

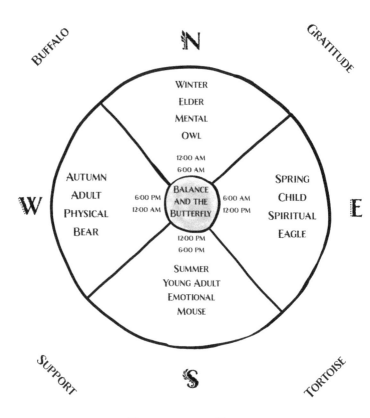

GRANDFATHER SKY

BUFFALO

GRATITUDE

N

WINTER
ELDER
MENTAL
OWL

12:00 AM
6:00 AM

AUTUMN
ADULT
PHYSICAL
BEAR

W

6:00 PM
12:00 AM

BALANCE
AND THE
BUTTERFLY

6:00 AM
12:00 PM

E

SPRING
CHILD
SPIRITUAL
EAGLE

12:00 PM
6:00 PM

SUMMER
YOUNG ADULT
EMOTIONAL
MOUSE

SUPPORT

S

TORTOISE

GRANDMOTHER EARTH

CHAPTER FIVE
THE CENTER AND THE BUTTERFLY

The butterfly is responsible for many of the events in the universe, simply by its flutter.

Direction: Center

Emphasis: Balance, connecting spiritual, emotional, physical, and mental faculties

Animal: Butterfly

Colors: White, Red, Yellow, and Black

The center of your Medicine Wheel gives you balance and a sense of stability. You may go to the center of your Medicine Wheel whenever you need balance in your life. The center of your Medicine Wheel is where all the faculties — spiritual, emotional, physical, and mental — connect. If all the faculties are in alignment, your Medicine Wheel will be a smooth ride; if not, your Medicine Wheel will become lopsided and take you off your true course. You know the importance of balance in your daily life, so you go to the center often. While the Northern Cheyenne Medicine Wheel does not specify an animal for the center, the butterfly, more than any other creature, embodies the journey of the Medicine Wheel by illustrating the complete cycle of life. This amazing creature reaches out and extends beauty and harmony to all it comes in contact with. You even see the colors of the Medicine Wheel — white, red, yellow, and black on most butterflies.

The appearance of the butterfly lightens the heart and the mind. Its sheer beauty and gentleness announce to the world its entrance. Everyone who comes in contact with a butterfly experiences a sense of joy and delight. You too bring this sense of joy and happiness to all the lives you touch throughout the day. This sublime creature of nature demonstrates the joy of movement and the powerful effect it has on those around it, and you exemplify this. The butterfly is responsible for many of the events in the universe, simply by its flutter.

TRAVEL LIGHT

The butterfly teaches you to live in moderation. Too much materialism is a heavy load to carry on your journey, so like the butterfly, you travel lightly. It makes the journey much easier with less worry. As the butterfly has the freedom to move in its immediate vicinity or to travel great distances, you too have a strong sense of freedom and flexibility because you are not bogged down with excess weight.

YOUR TRANSFORMATION IS BEAUTIFUL

The life of a butterfly begins when the female butterfly lays her eggs on the leaf of a tree. This is called the embryonic stage and is similar to the eastern quadrant of your Medicine Wheel. After a few days, the caterpillar hatches from the egg and eats and eats and eats. This is known as the larval stage. This phase takes place in the southern quadrant of your Medicine Wheel. The next phase is where the greatest transformation takes place when the caterpillar attaches itself to a tree and begins to form a hard shell called the chrysalis. This stage correlates with the western quadrant of your Medicine Wheel, the resting or hiding stage. After several weeks or months, the butterfly emerges and becomes the creature nature intended it to be. The emergence of the butterfly takes place during the final stage of your Medicine Wheel in the northern quadrant.

You have gone through all the stages of the Medicine Wheel and have been transformed into the divine person that nature intended you to be. Like the butterfly that started out in the early embryonic stages, then developed into the caterpillar, and then developed into the mature butterfly, you too have undergone dramatic changes from the moment you set out to accomplish your life's purpose. Like the caterpillar that hides under the leaf and is transformed during the chrysalis stage and then emerges as a butterfly, you too have evolved into a new creature. You don't know how this happened, it just happened. The transformation that took place within you becomes a dynamic force that pulsates out to the world around you just like the spokes on your Medicine Wheel.

Your transformation is beautiful. Sometimes you don't even recognize yourself. Like the spokes of the Medicine Wheel, you radiate beauty out to all those around you. The beauty that you exude is not necessarily a physical beauty, although it could be, but it is much deeper than that. Your beauty is in the kindness and compassion of your speech, your written word, and your actions. This is what it means to be a truly beautiful person. Beauty on the outside quickly fades, but inner beauty is continually being renewed.

Before the caterpillar transforms into the butterfly, it becomes a gooey mass, totally unrecognizable as a caterpillar or butterfly. After time, the gooey mass takes shape and the butterfly begins to form. That's the metamorphosis. That's what it means to become a new creature. Whenever you are in the midst of creating something new and unique you will go through your own personal metamorphosis. This is where faith comes in — faith in yourself and what you can accomplish. The chrysalis stage is a very powerful stage where you begin to believe in yourself and what you can achieve.

This does not happen overnight, but over time. For some, the transformation will take years; slow growth is always the best. As long as you are keeping the laws of nature and abiding by right living, your metamorphosis will take place. It is an amazing feeling.

Once the butterfly breaks through the chrysalis stage, it enters into the final stage of maturation. The butterfly emerges, spreads its wings, and takes flight. The butterfly's wings extend out to all the quadrants of the Wheel and bring balance.

All the phases of the butterfly's transformation are part of the Medicine Wheel. Each phase is a necessary step towards maturity. Just as in your life, these phases must go from child to young adult, adult, and then elder. This process happens automatically. You don't decide to learn life's lessons; they appear right in front of you. It is a wondrous and magical experience and it happens all the time. Every experience is a glorious opportunity for growth and change. You have the potential for unbridled possibilities and unlimited promise. The butterfly teaches you that no matter where you are in your life, you can change and become something new.

And now that you have reached this state, you are able to extend yourself out to others. This will be done almost effortlessly because you are relying on the Creator for inspiration, energy, and force.

The incredible journey of the Medicine Wheel is not done yet. You still have a few more steps along the journey, but you are almost home. You have become a new creature, but there are a few more things left for you to learn on your Medicine Wheel journey.

BELOW

GRANDMOTHER EARTH

SUPPORT

TORTOISE

CHAPTER SIX
GRANDMOTHER EARTH
AND THE TORTOISE

While very beautiful and ornate, the tortoise's shell is very practical. It provides excellent protection from intense heat and high temperatures.

Direction: Below

Emphasis: Providing support for all living creatures

Animal: Tortoise

Color: Green

Now you will enter a different dimension of your Medicine Wheel; different from the four cardinal directions since it addresses what lies beneath you. It is the foundation you stand on, the ground on which you walk. It is the power of Grandmother Earth. Not only does Grandmother Earth provide you with support, but she also provides you with the nourishment that sustains your life. The Earth is your birthplace and your resting place. It is where you came from and eventually where you will return. The animal that helps you at this stage of your journey is the tortoise. The color most associated with Grandmother Earth is green, the color of vegetation. The color green represents energy and growth. You wear green when you want to project freshness and newness.

Grandmother Earth is all around you providing you with a beautiful environment in which to grow and learn. The magnificent mountain ranges, identified by up and down formations, symbolize the earth's heartbeat, reminding you that the earth is a living, breathing entity. The sandy beaches, the meadows, and the fields all give you warmth and repose. The rocks and the cliffs remind you of strength and endurance. The oceans, lakes, and rivers remind you that nature is in a constant state of flow. Grandmother Earth makes a powerful statement with the eruption of volcanoes, symbolizing the tremendous forces within.

SOIL IS SACRED

Probably the most important substance that Grandmother Earth provides is the soil. It is what you build on, the substance that your food grows from. The soil holds your water and provides vitamins and nourishment for plants and animals. In the Native American tradition, the soil is sacred. It is used in sacred healing ceremonies as a balm for ailments and illnesses. Psychologically, the soil provides a playground for adults. Just playing in the soil has regenerative, almost immediate, benefits for eliminating worry and anxiety. Did you plant a garden at the beginning of your

Medicine Wheel journey? How is it looking now? Have you been working in your garden throughout your Medicine Wheel journey? When was the last time you got down on your hands and knees and worked in the soil? Society teaches us that dirt is something we want to wash away, get rid of; yet playing in the dirt can bring about healing and comfort. It can also be very calming and relaxing. In addition to the mental, physical, and emotional benefits, gardening and working outdoors is a wonderful way to honor Grandmother Earth. When you honor nature, nature will respond and honor you.

Grasslands, wetlands, forests, and prairies provide a habitat for nature's wildlife. The creatures living in the ocean and the entire animal kingdom are dependent on Grandmother Earth for survival. Humans have a huge responsibility to care for Grandmother Earth since our entire livelihood depends on her. This is the part of the journey where you take responsibility for the earth and for all those creatures large and small living on it. Your life extends far beyond yourself and you start to build a web that connects you with all living creatures.

MAKE INTEGRITY PART OF YOUR MISSION

When you think of the earth as your grandmother, the need to care for her becomes personal. There are numerous ways to help care for Grandmother Earth and here you will bring your own special touch. Whether it is recycling, converting to solar power, using less fuel, or conserving water, you have a special part to play in caring for Grandmother Earth. You will seek out agencies, non-profit organizations, corporations, and small businesses whose mission is to care for the earth and find ways to work with them. The more you bring health and healing to Grandmother Earth the more you will experience health and healing in your own life.

In addition to providing you with health and nourishment, Grandmother Earth provides you with a foundation to stand on, but what do you stand for? This is the time to dig deep down into your soul and discover your core values that will serve as the foundation of your entire existence. What do you bring up from the depths of your being? What are your guiding principles? What principles are integral to your personal beliefs and your business dealings? You know that none of your plans will work if you are not basing them on a foundation of integrity. In your personal life, you want lasting friendships and strong family ties, so your dealings with friends and family members are always built on the principle of integrity. In your business dealings, you want what's best for your clients because that will make your reputation and your business grow, so you make integrity part of your mission.

SET YOUR OWN PACE; CREATE YOUR OWN STYLE

The animal associated with Grandmother Earth is the tortoise. From the deserts in the southwestern United States to the Mediterranean grasslands to the rocky Galapagos Islands, the tortoise makes its home and adapts quite nicely to the environment that Grandmother Earth provides. Always close to the ground, the tortoise finds nourishment in leaves, fruits, flowers, grasses, weeds, and vegetables.

The tortoise sets its own pace. It moves very slowly. Its body doesn't allow quick movement. Tortoises go about their day quietly, peacefully, unharmed by events or setbacks. They live very long lives. Some can live to 150 years.

You, like the tortoise, don't allow events and circumstances to upset your schedule. You move about your day with a peaceful presence even in the midst of chaos. Things outside of yourself never cause you to erupt because you know that these outside circumstances are only temporary. Because you move at your own pace, or rather the pace that nature intended for you, you are always on time and you never have to rush. When you rush, you give the impression that you are not in control, so you never rush. Even if you are late, it is perfect timing. You are in sync with nature, not someone else's clock. And the amazing thing is that you are always on time. It is incredible how that works out.

The most unique feature of the tortoise is its shell. While very beautiful and ornate, the tortoise's shell is very practical. It provides excellent protection from intense heat and high temperatures. The tortoise can withstand extreme temperatures up to 115 degrees Fahrenheit. You too, can withstand the heat. Whatever stressful situation you encounter, you deal with it using composure and tact.

There will be other times when you will have to endure intense coldness and loneliness. Like the tortoise that endures the long, cold winter nights, you too, will have times when you will be given the cold shoulder or be ostracized by those around you. Like the tortoise, you endure the cold, freezing temperatures because you know that it will only last a nightfall and then the sun will come out and shine on you again. Tortoises do not control their environment, they adapt to it. You do the same. Whether you experience intense heat or freezing cold, you adapt to it. That is the reason for the hard shell.

The tortoise's shell also protects it from predators. Whenever the tortoise is threatened it retreats inward where it is safe and sound. Its shell is impossible to break. Like the tortoise, no matter how hard someone tries to crack your shell, you will not allow it. Your tough outer shell can't be penetrated by negative comments or criticisms. Instead they boomerang back to the person who initiated them. The person speaking in such a manner doesn't know the truth, therefore they condemn themselves. Their words are always in-effective because they are not living in truth. They are living in fear and anxiety, which causes them to lash out at you. But you don't pay any attention. What they say has no impact on you. Like the tortoise, you find refuge in your shell where nothing can touch you.

The tortoise's shell allows it to crawl into wedges between rock formations, and you too will learn how to hide when you sense danger. Grandmother Earth provides hiding places for those whose lives are being threatened. Your predator will walk right past you as you lie silently between the rocks. You will outwit the cleverest of your enemies by hiding in plain sight.

Every tortoise's shell has its own unique design and you, too, have your own unique style and signature. You may be wearing clothes from the nearest thrift shop, but your style is impeccable. Your clothes, shoes, and accessories are unique. No one can put it together like you. No matter where you are, you look the part. It's not just your clothes; it's your poise and presence that make you stand out. Whatever you are wearing, you project an air of dignity and you command respect.

YOUR LIFE'S DISTINCT PATTERN

On a deeper level, your life has its own distinct pattern just like the pattern on the tortoise's shell. This pattern begins to emerge over the years and will give you direction when embarking on a new project. Try this little exercise. Start from your birth and identify major changes, shifts, and events in your life. This can be a list, a timeline, a spiral, whatever art form you choose. Then fill in relationships, jobs, moves, educational achievements, major purchases, important dates — whatever you see as meaningful in your life. Even if the events are painful, still include them in your pattern. By identifying painful experiences and when they have occurred you can avoid them in the future. So don't ignore them; they are part of your pattern. Once you have filled in as many events as possible, you will see a pattern emerge. Do you see a change every two years or three years? Do you see yourself repeating activities? Can you match up events that seem to recur every few years without any prompting from you?

Once you identify the particular pattern in your life, you can use it to chart your next move. This is a very valuable tool and unique to each individual. You will begin to see your future by understanding your past. When your dreams and ambitions are in alignment with your life's pattern, they will manifest. It's that simple. If you seem to be spinning your wheels and knocking your head against a brick wall, you might not be in alignment with your life's pattern.

Because of your unique pattern, you never, ever compare your life to someone else's. We all tend to look at what someone else has and want what they have, but this is a major distraction and draws you away from your full potential. You don't know what lies ahead in someone else's life, or what they have endured in the past, so you never envy them. You stay focused on your own life and your true purpose.

TO THE RESCUE

The tortoise can have its setbacks, literally. Tortoises can slip, fall, and end up on their backs. This can be deadly, but when a tortoise sees another tortoise that has flipped over, it comes to the rescue and helps the overturned one get back up on its feet. It is amazing to see how they do this. Sometimes two or three are involved in helping the tortoise regain its natural state. If along the road of life, you come upon someone who is laid up on their back like the tortoise, you do all you can to help them get back on their feet. We all have a responsibility to help those in need. You too can lose your balance from a fall or from slipping and sliding and be laid up for a while waiting for someone to come along and help you get back on your feet. So when you see someone in a desperate situation, you step in immediately and help them up. We all fall on hard times and you never know when it could happen to you, so you are always ready to come to the rescue and save the day for someone else. In some cases, you might end up saving a life!

This is why you build strong relationships with family members, friends, and co-workers. They provide you with support. You surround yourself with friends and family who support your ideas, your vision, and your growth because you know that when someone supports what you are doing, you can accomplish amazing things. When you are having doubts, you go to those people who will encourage and cheer you on. And just as your friends and family have supported you, you also provide support and comfort for them.

In addition to surrounding yourself with people who are supportive, you surround yourself with objects and items that are positive and uplifting. You bring in things from the outdoors to enhance your home. Flowers, pine cones, plants, bowls of fruit make your home happy and healthy. You surround yourself with nature, adding to the beauty of your home and the well-being of your body, mind, and soul.

STAND YOUR GROUND

While the tortoise is compassionate and caring, it also stands its ground. If it feels threatened, it snaps. If someone invades your territory, or gets even a little too close, it's okay to snap at them. It isn't deadly; it's just a warning to the other person to take a few steps back. It doesn't have to be harsh, just a quick, innocuous snap. They will get the message and they will respect you more for standing your ground.

Since the tortoise spends its life so close to the ground, it is in tune with the sensitivities of Grandmother Earth. At this time in your Medicine Wheel journey, you might feel the impulse to visit a sacred spot. There are sacred places in the United States and around the world that have strong magnetic fields under them. These magnetic fields are powerful and can influence your life long after you have visited them and walked them. Going on a sacred journey to one of these places identifies you with the tortoise. Once you find the magnetic field that has attracted you, walk it slowly, like the tortoise. The benefits of a pilgrimage like this will be astounding.

You might decide to visit Sedona, Big Horn Medicine Wheel, the Grand Canyon, Yosemite, or Mount Shasta. Bear Butte in the Black Hills of South Dakota; Chimayo, New Mexico; and Mount McKinley are also sacred places that may ignite a powerful force within you. Take in the subtle, yet powerful message that Grandmother Earth has especially for you and then apply it to your life.

And now it is time for you to look up! Grandfather Sky has much to bestow on you!

ABOVE

GRANDFATHER SKY

GIVING

BUFFALO

CHAPTER SEVEN
GRANDFATHER SKY
AND THE BUFFALO

It has been said that when the Natives prayed for food, the buffalo would hear the prayer and move in the direction of that prayer. The buffalo would sacrifice himself for the survival of the people.

Direction: Above

Emphasis: Giving, forgiving

Animal: Buffalo

Color: Blue

As Grandmother Earth supports you from below, Grandfather Sky guides and protects you from above. Grandfather Sky gives you sunshine and warmth during the day and the stars and the moon to light up the night. Clouds and rainbows sprawl across the sky with meaning and messages. The animal that guides you and protects you on this part of your Medicine Wheel journey is the buffalo. The color is blue, the color of serenity and peace.

No matter what happens in the world, the Creator has surrounded the earth with peace and tranquility. Wherever you are on the planet, you can look up and feel the safety and calmness of the light blue sky above. The majestic sunrise and the soothing sunset sprawled across the sky are matched in beauty only by the magnificent, voluminous clouds that Grandfather Sky uses to adorn the horizon. The clouds are a gentle reminder that no two days will ever be the same. There will always be sudden conflicts, stressful situations, and unforeseen circumstances that will shape your day and like the clouds, they too will pass. Grandfather Sky teaches you that all is temporary.

CLOUDS: PROBLEMS OR PROSPERITY?

On a more practical level, the clouds teach you how to deal with picayune incidentals and minor obstacles that get thrown in your way all the time. Throughout life, almost on a daily basis, you will encounter small aggravations. Whether they originate from the people you live with or the people you work with, you will have to deal with nagging irritations on a continual basis. These are not the big issues — divorce, cancer, bankruptcy, or death of a loved one. These are the daily common annoyances that can drive you crazy. They can keep you up at night and give you a headache in the morning if you let them get to you, but the clouds give you an exit strategy. Temporary cloud formations teach you that your tiny annoyances will be gone in a day or two, in some cases a week; they don't last. Like a cloud, they are light and will float away on their own. Try this out. The next time something really annoys you, write it down. Then go back to it a week later. You will probably already have forgotten about it and you will wonder why you got so annoyed in the first place.

But you don't have to wait a week or longer to get relief. There is another way to tackle your daily dilemmas. That is to set your mind on another cloud, another situation, one that you can tackle using your brains and brawn. Once you focus on another situation, the petty incidental that was gnawing away at you will disappear, like a cloud. That's how that works. Whenever a small, yet annoying event springs up, you conquer it by focusing on another "cloud," preferably one of greater significance. It is a mind game. You trick your mind into focusing on another more pressing "problem cloud," so that the first one doesn't bother you anymore. The lesson is to not let the small incidentals throw you off your game. Use the smaller incidentals as a boost to set your mind on something more important. With all the daily annoyances that come in your direction, you will have plenty of opportunity to practice this technique. Every time a petty event occurs you will know how to react and use it to your advantage. This secret strategy will literally uplift and motivate you to always set your mind on something greater. Grandfather Sky reminds you to set your mind on things above. You don't get bogged down in petty annoyances. You continually raise your thoughts above it all. The air is lighter up there and you aren't weighted down by people's ignorance. Plus, you move much faster when you place yourself above it all.

Clouds also contain messages and meanings as individual as each person on the planet. As you drive to work in the morning or head home at night you might want to stop and take a moment to gaze up at the clouds and look for the hidden messages they contain that can guide you through your life. Let your imagination run wild and soon you will see patterns emerge in the clouds with counsel and meaning meant just for you. Just like the patterns you found on the tortoise's back, you will also find patterns in the sky; it's nature's method of communication.

Clouds also provide a magical, mystical experience. Remember the time you had a window seat on an airplane that flew through the clouds and you felt like you touched a piece of heaven? Or do you remember the time when a fog cloud enveloped your walk to the office? The little tiny droplets of moisture created a mystical experience that took you out of the material realm and put your life in a different perspective.

You may come in contact with dark clouds. Dark clouds warn you of storms ahead. Be vigilant to circumstances that alert you to trouble or danger that might be coming in your direction. You have the insight to avert a catastrophe before it happens. When you do this, people will admire your quick thinking and your ability to avoid disaster.

Grandfather Sky also fills the sky with rain clouds, the symbol of prosperity and abundance. You look forward to rainy days because they are a reminder of the good fortune Grandfather Sky is going to send you. If you are fortunate, Grandfather Sky will decorate the landscape with one of nature's most beautiful ornaments, the rainbow, symbolizing a promising future ahead. You look up at the rainbow and you embrace your future and anticipate all good things.

And when the night comes, you gaze up at the majesty of the stars. Throughout the centuries, stars have played an important part in the direction of people's lives. When the journey gets too hard, the stars reach down from the heavens and give hope to all of humanity. All you have to do is anticipate and the stars will lead you to where you want to go.

And the moon, which continually changes its shape and color — sometimes a slight crescent, and sometimes a glowing full moon — is always there to assist. The moon's illumination reminds you that it is never totally dark; even in your darkest night there will still be a light to get you through till the morning.

THE ACT OF GIVING

Grandfather Sky teaches you the act of giving. Remember when you learned in science class that plants breathe in carbon dioxide and exhale oxygen, and humans breathe in oxygen and exhale carbon dioxide? That same type of symbiotic relationship is repeated over and over again throughout nature. You can apply this same concept to your own life and benefit from nature's rhythm. As you give to others, your arms open wide and you are in a position to receive all that Grandfather Sky has to give you.

Throughout your Medicine Wheel journey you will be involved in a series of exchanges where you will provide something for someone and they will provide something back, but first you need to take stock of your own skills and talents and determine who can benefit from them. This might take a while to figure out — months, even years — but you will discover that you have multiple talents that can be applied to any number of situations. Then find good, honest people who need what you have and offer it to them. That is how you open the door of giving and receiving.

It sounds like basic economics, but this is far more personal. It doesn't have to be an exchange of money. It can be ideas, contacts, energy, positive words that you give away. Even a smile can make a difference in a person's day. Get creative and think of all the "non-monetary" contributions you can make to the world that sometimes can have a bigger impact than writing out a check. It can be as simple as a telephone conversation that brings cheer and hope to someone in the hospital, or it can be a new way of doing things at the office that saves time and money. There are an infinite number of ways to help humanity. Your skills and talents are vital in that process, but always remember that you are offering your gifts and talents to Grandfather Sky, not necessarily to the person you interact with, even though he or she will directly benefit. You never have to keep tabs on anyone because it is Grandfather Sky who will repay you. It might not come back to you the way you intended, but it will come back to you.

Another great strategy to use for giving and receiving is to be the one in the middle — the "middleman" or "middle woman." If you can bring two people together for the benefit of both, that increases your reservoir even more. Find the skills and talents of one person and match them up with the needs of another, and both will be appreciative of your efforts. The more you network and increase your web of contacts, the more you will be able to help others.

THE ACT OF SACRIFICE

While all this is good, there is a deeper, more profound level of giving and that is the act of sacrifice, the highest and most noble act known to humanity. And this is where the buffalo comes in. While all animals are sacred in Native traditions, the buffalo holds a special place in Native American culture and spirituality. It has been said that when the Natives prayed for food, the buffalo would hear the prayer and move in the direction of that prayer. The buffalo would sacrifice itself for the survival of the people. The buffalo was willing to have its body used on earth for the greatest good before entering the spirit world. It was the supreme act of sacrifice. No part of the buffalo was ever wasted. Buffalo hides were used for teepees, clothing, and blankets. The bones were shaped into utensils, the teeth were used for jewelry and the meat of the buffalo was the main substance of survival.

Sacrifice is a hard concept for most to embrace, but you embrace it willingly. You know that the practice of sacrifice ultimately leads to new life, so you offer your life up in service to others. But how is this actually accomplished? Must you physically die to help others? No, this is not a physical death. Although some are called to martyrdom, this is the death of the ego. The way to do this is through giving of the self. This is the process of becoming who you really are. You won't truly know who you are until you know your capacity to give. You don't give from your surplus, but you sacrifice that which is important to you and you don't expect anything in return. You learn to do this first with those closest to you — your family and friends. You learn to give to them and to put their interests above your own.

Then, your giving extends beyond those you love and you begin to give to those beyond your immediate circle. You look for ways to help others, a helping hand, a gesture, but it is always done out of love, not out of duty. You give because you truly want to give. You want to experience the outpouring of love because only then will your heart be filled with it. Every time you give to others, a small part of your ego dies. Sacrificing, putting someone else's desires ahead of yours, is the act of dying. Every time you do this, something is born inside of you and your existence rises to a new level of being and understanding. Eventually, your small acts of kindness will grow into larger acts and your mind will explode with a multitude of ways to help other people.

While sacrifice is the greatest act one can perform for humanity, you never throw your pearls to the swine. Never. You recognize and value your own unique gifts that you have to give to the world and you give them wisely. Sacrifice is something that you choose to do for the greater good. You never want to place yourself in an abusive relationship and think that it is sacrifice. No, that is only insanity. There are some people who will want to take advantage of your goodness, but stay alert and determine how your sacrifice will have the greatest impact.

THE ACT OF FORGIVING

There is another form of giving that is an integral part of your Medicine Wheel journey and that is the act of forgiving. It is through forgiveness that we experience our true soul power. Whatever someone did or said that was hurtful, it must be forgiven. Then you will experience the power of new life and you will be able to accomplish things beyond your wildest imagination. Forgiveness is a big part of the creative process.

Forgiveness is not easy and not fast and, in some cases, it may even seem impossible, but you begin the process by wanting to forgive. It can be a very dark, lonely time, almost unbearable, but in the depths of despair, lightning strikes from above and you are given the strength to forgive. Forgiveness can be a powerful vehicle to help you accomplish your true purpose. Forgiveness gives you freedom from the past and control over your future. You are no longer bound by someone else's evil actions. You can move forward in the world with grace from above.

It is natural to want to retaliate and seek revenge on someone who has done you wrong. It takes great strength of character to refrain from it, especially in a society that seems to evoke and encourage it on all levels. We live in a society where the one who "evens the score" becomes the hero, the role model, the person we want to be like, but that just fuels the ego, the one thing you are trying to eliminate. Never think for a moment that the person who offended you gets away with it. Nature has something in store for them that fits their actions exactly, so you don't have to take revenge on anyone or retaliate. Besides, revenge is never satisfied. The ego will always want more. Once you begin to retaliate against someone, the more your ego will tell you to keep going; the road of retaliation is never-ending. You will end up causing more destruction to yourself than your enemy. You're too good for that. You will never let an enemy control your emotions or your actions. You don't entangle yourself in anyone else's wrongdoing. You don't retaliate. You don't seek revenge. All you have to do is wait. The Creator never rewards evil behavior and their actions will come back to them in ways you never could have imagined or orchestrated. If you execute any form of revenge you are just going to mess things up. Just wait.

It is easy to be nice to the person in the salon or the grocery store, but when a co-worker undermines your project, or manipulates your work environment, it is very difficult to respond with kindness. It takes a trained mind to be able to override the fight-or-flight reaction. When you are being attacked or threatened, blood rushes from your brain to your arms and your legs, so your natural biological instinct is fight or run away. This fight-or-flight reaction can take on many forms. You can fight back with fists, emails, negative speech, or gossip. This eventually leads to bitterness, vindictiveness, and hostility. Or you can go in the opposite direction and run away, but that doesn't solve anything because wherever you run to, the same problem will occur. It's cliché, but true: you can run, but you can't hide. There is an alternative to the fight-or-flight response and that is to forgive and turn the injustice into something meaningful and purposeful. Whatever obstacle someone has thrown at you, it can be used to move your life forward and upward. That is the power of the Medicine Wheel. It takes great discipline and self-control to resist fighting back, but you learned self-discipline from the mouse in the second quadrant so you know you can do it.

You will be given the opportunity over and over again to develop a steadfast response to negative situations. Your aim is for all your actions to be positive and good, especially when you are mistreated. When people wrong you, you don't fight back; you take the high road. That is what it means to practice forgiveness. It doesn't mean that you don't have to defend yourself, but you have to ask yourself if it's worth it. You don't let any pettiness come into your being. You don't go to their level. It's okay to speak your mind and stand up for yourself, but you never want to say something that you will regret later on down the line. Once you have stated your case, walk away with your head held high and your dignity intact. Just know that the Creator has something greater for you to do.

Sometimes you don't have to respond at all. Sometimes ignoring someone is the best response. That is the ultimate snub. Instead of speaking your mind, save the energy and channel it into something worthwhile. Every time you think about an injustice done to you, let it motivate you to do positive things. As for the person responsible for the injustice, they have already set themselves up for their own downfall. Do nothing and just watch what nature has in store for them. It might take years, but nature will repay. And just know that the Creator has something good in store for you.

Many times, when you find yourself in an unfair situation it is really nature's way of getting your attention — to force you to remove yourself from that situation and to find a place where your skills and talents will be recognized. Because you have forgiven, your compassion and understanding will grow and you will attract kindhearted people like yourself. This is all part of the act of forgiveness.

Lastly, you will have to practice the act of forgiving yourself. Throughout your Medicine Wheel journey, you will do things that were not in your best interest and you will find yourself stuck in a pattern of thought — 'why did I do that?' or 'what was I thinking?' This is when you practice the act of forgiving yourself. You are not helping anyone by going over the mistakes of your past. It is the wrong use of the memory anyway. Forgiveness is never easy, especially when you have to forgive yourself, but in time you will be released from your human flaws and frailty and you will be able to use the experience to help others who are going through something similar.

BEGINNING AGAIN

Once you have given all you can of yourself and forgiven those around you as well as yourself, then you are empty and you are able to receive even greater things in your life. Then your Medicine Wheel journey will begin again, but this time your journey will take on a much deeper meaning. You are no longer thinking primarily about yourself, but you are thinking about others. Every time you take the Medicine Wheel journey it becomes less and less about yourself and more and more about others.

You will experience all seven directions of the Medicine Wheel several times throughout your life and each time you will graduate to a new level of learning. Through it all you will learn to balance your spiritual, emotional, physical, and mental activities. You take your life's mission seriously, you develop your skills and talents, you give thanks for all that you have been given, and lastly you offer your services up for the good of humanity. Each time you do this you will get closer and closer to your true self.

And then one day, your Medicine Wheel will start to slow down and you will wonder what is happening. You understand so much of life and you want to keep going, but your Medicine Wheel is doing something different. Since the Medicine Wheel has always sent you in the right direction, you slowly follow its lead.

CHAPTER EIGHT
THE END OF THE ROAD
AND THE COYOTE

*In Native American tradition, the coyote is the
trickster. His message is clear and simple:
no matter what you are going through in life don't
take yourself too seriously.
Take time to laugh and see the humor of it all.*

Direction: End of the Road

Emphasis: Understanding the riddles of life

Animal: Coyote

Color: Whatever you want it to be

Your Medicine Wheel is always on time and always brings you to your destination. There are no shortcuts; no cutting corners, you arrive at exactly the right time and the right place. There were times when your Medicine Wheel may have gone off the right road, but you quickly got back on track. There may have been times when your Medicine Wheel got stuck, but you managed to get it going again. And then there were those times when your Medicine Wheel went in reverse, but you quickly changed directions and got your bearings back. For the most part, you did your best to stay on the right road. There were times when it was smooth and easy traveling and then there were some bumps along the way, a couple of detours, but your Medicine Wheel always got you to where you were supposed to be. You traveled many places you never thought imaginable, you learned lessons that left a permanent imprint on your spirit, and you brought joy and happiness to those you met along the way.

While there have been many animals to guide you along your journey, one animal has been with you the entire time. He is the coyote. In Native American tradition, the coyote is the trickster. His message is clear and simple: no matter what you are going through in life, don't take yourself too seriously. Take time to laugh and see the humor of it all. Keep smiling. It will keep you young and healthy.

You will find the coyote throughout your Medicine Wheel journey, but he never stays for too long and he always keeps his distance. He can show up at any time, any season, any quadrant, any direction. Coyote will sometimes show up at one of your most difficult times to remind you to see the humor in it. The coyote teaches you to laugh and lighten up. The coyote helps you to understand the riddles of life and make sense out of any situation.

FOLLOW THE COYOTE

Then there will come a time when the coyote will show up and it will be different from all other times. In the past, his appearance reminded you to laugh and lighten up, but now he is very serious. Your Medicine Wheel has come to a complete stop and the coyote is standing in the distance begging you to follow him. This is unusual because you have never followed him before. You couldn't follow him before because your Medicine Wheel was always leading you in a different direction, but now you must leave your Medicine Wheel and follow the coyote. At first you don't want to leave your Medicine Wheel because it has been a part of your life for so long and you don't think you can travel without it, but you can. You see the coyote going further into the distance. Your curiosity gets the best of you and you start to follow him. The coyote stops and waits for you to catch up. Even though you don't know where you are going you are not afraid. As you move towards the coyote, he goes deeper and deeper into the forest. It is a bit odd because you are going into unknown territory, yet you have no fear, you have only curiosity to know where the coyote is taking you. You feel a tingling sensation that tells you something magical is about to happen.

As you get further and further from your Medicine Wheel, you hear the faint voices of your loved ones in the background, but the coyote urges you to pay no attention to them. The voices get fainter and fainter. You want to look back, but the coyote tells you to keep your eyes on him only or you will get lost. You follow the coyote deeper and deeper into the forest until you hear the voices no more. You are engulfed by silence and you wonder where the coyote is leading you, because you have never been here before. It is a place of peace and tranquility and you wonder why you never followed the coyote in the past, but you are glad you are following him now. Then the silence is broken and you hear a pop — as though someone popped a champagne bottle. You look around and try to adjust to what just happened. You are still in a fog and then it dawns on you that you just crossed over into another dimension. You have never experienced anything like this before. You suddenly realize that it was all just a dream — the dream of Creation. Everything about the Medicine Wheel seemed so real and now you realize it was all just a dream and you wonder why you took everything so seriously to begin with. You feel like the coyote played the ultimate trick on you and then in the distance you hear laughter. You feel as though the whole world is laughing at you and then you recognize the voices. You have heard those voices before, but it was a long time ago. You recognize them as your loved ones who have gone before you and gone through their own trials and tribulations — grief and sorrow, pain and suffering just like you did — all to learn life's lessons. And you, just like they, are victorious! You did it! You accomplished what you were meant to accomplish. You fulfilled your life's purpose. Now all the pain and sorrow you experienced is not even a memory. It's gone forever. You only take with you the joy and happiness that you brought to others. You realize that it was all worth it. And that's what makes you laugh. Your laughter continues. You know that you accomplished what the world needed. You did your part.

You can't stop laughing. It was a great ride and you can hardly wait for that spectacular day when you see your loved ones who are still on their Medicine Wheel journey walk through the forest the same way you did. You will watch their faces light up when they recognize your laughter and they, too, will know that they have accomplished what they were meant to accomplish.

Coyote teaches, "Don't take yourself so seriously." Humor is the final element to the Medicine Wheel. One needs to play and to laugh. It is only a game anyway and soon you will put all your toys away and go back to the Creator when he determines that you have accomplished all you were meant to accomplish. Then your real life will begin. You will look back at all you did and realize it was all just a dream — a magical experience that seemed so real, so intense. And then suddenly it all goes Poof! And you're gone! That's the magic of your Medicine Wheel.